MAKING

CHRISTMAS
SCRAPBOOKS

Joy Aitman

Rosie's
First Christmas
1995
we spent our first
Christmas together
in Scotland with
Granny & Grampa
Kirsty & Stacey
Emily
Uncle Paul

SEARCH PRESS

First published in Great Britain 2005

Search Press Limited
Wellwood, North Farm Road,
Tunbridge Wells, Kent TN2 3DR

Text copyright © Joy Aitman 2005

Photographs by Roddy Paine Photographic Studios

Photographs and design copyright © Search Press Ltd. 2005

ISBN 1 84448 068 2

The Publishers and author can accept no responsibility for any
consequences arising from the information, advice or
instructions given in this publication.

Suppliers
If you have difficulty in obtaining any of the materials and
equipment mentioned in this book, then please visit the
Search Press website for details of suppliers:
www.searchpress.com

Alternatively, you can write to the Publishers at the address
above, for a current list of stockists, including firms who
operate a mail-order service.

Publishers' note
All the step-by-step photographs in this book feature the
author, Joy Aitman, demonstrating how to make
scrapbook pages. No models have been used.

Manufactured by Universal Graphics Pte Ltd, Singapore

Printed in Malaysia by Times Offset (M) Sdn Bhd

*Dedicated to the memory of my brother
Nicholas, our Christmas day baby, with
whom I spent twenty-four wonderful
Christmases, and to the rest of my
family with whom I know I will enjoy
many more.*

Acknowledgements
I would like to thank:
*Mark, Rosie, Jake, Gracie and Duncan for
letting me take so many photographs of them and
allowing me so much time to scrapbook
and write.*
*Joanne and Hilary for putting up with my
creative mess!*
Sophie, Roz and Juan for all their help.
Martin and Caroline for their enthusiasm.
*Benno White at Roddy Paine Photographic
Studios for the photography.*

Cover
Noel
See page 23.

Page 1
Rosie's first Christmas
I have embellished this page using Christmas decorations.

Opposite
Give
This simple page has been decorated with stickers.

Contents

Introduction

My love of photography and my interest in crafts led me into the wonderful hobby of scrapbooking five years ago. I take lots of photographs all year round but I take the most at Christmas, my favourite time of year. I also have many photographs of my own childhood Christmas celebrations. The colours, the smells, the traditions – they all beg to be scrapbooked.

Christmas photographs are particularly difficult to take. The lighting might be poor, flash photography bleaches the colours, and the subjects can be overexcited or uncooperative. Year after year, too, the photographs tend to look similar – the subjects are a year older, but there are all the standard scenes: putting up the tree, opening the presents, the school Nativity play, lighting the Christmas pudding. For all these reasons, you might struggle to find the inspiration you need to create your scrapbooking pages.

That is where this book comes in! Since I, too, find that I am working with similar photographs every year, I decided that I needed to try out some new techniques for my Christmas layouts and also to think a little 'out of the box' when designing. I have come up with a mixture of these ideas and techniques to share with you, to help you to scrapbook your Christmas memories.

Opposite
Capture every aspect of Christmas on your layouts. Don't forget to take pictures inside and outside.

Materials

The materials for scrapbooking must be of archival quality and photo-safe to preserve your photographs. Albums, card, paper, pens and adhesives must be acid free. Acid causes the paper itself to deteriorate and also migrates into photographs, turning them yellow, brittle and faded. Acidic adhesives can eat away the emulsion from photographs. Paper should also be lignin free, since lignin causes the paper to brown and crumble. Always buy from well-known scrapbooking companies.

Basic equipment

A personal trimmer or **guillotine** makes cropping your photographs quicker and easier, eliminating wobbly edges caused by scissors. They are safe for children to use.

Scissors should be comfortable and suitable for the task. I use a small, sharp pair for cutting around lettering or small shapes and a larger pair for general cutting.

A **craft knife** has a number of uses. I particularly like to use one for cutting out titles. Make sure it is retractable or has a safety cover. You will need to use it with a **cutting mat.** Choose a mat with a grid on it as this will make cutting and measuring easier.

A **corner rounder** is a useful tool. I like to use one when I am making tags or labels.

It is important to choose the correct **adhesive** for the job. Double-sided **photo stickers** or **tape** are suitable for photographs. So is **repositionable tape,** which comes on a runner. It is useful for attaching items temporarily and becomes permanent if left. Never use a wet adhesive for photographs. **Glue dots** are essential for sticking down heavy embellishments. A **glue pen** or **glue stick** is handy for small paper items such as punched shapes. **PVA glue** is a good strong adhesive, useful for sticking down the paper when you are covering books or journals.

Pens, used for journaling or decorating pages, should be acid free, waterproof and fade resistant. It is useful to have a selection of calligraphy, fine point, brush and dot pens.

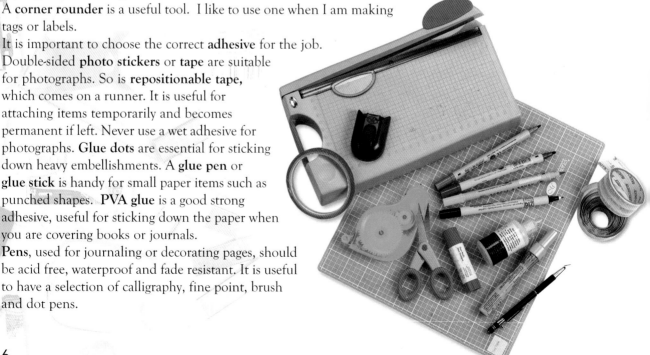

A guillotine, corner rounder, cutting mat, pens, glue dots and photo stickers, craft knife, glue pen, PVA glue, glue stick, scissors, repositionable tape runner and pink double-sided tape.

Albums

Albums should be acid free and sturdy. They come in a number of different styles and sizes but there are three basic types.

Ring-bound albums are very basic. They contain top-loading page protectors, which you fill with your finished layouts. They cannot be extended in any way.

Strap-bound albums are pages connected with flexible straps. You work directly on to the pages and then cover them with slip-over protectors. They can be extended by threading more pages on to the strap.

Post-bound albums contain page protectors bound together with two to three screw posts. You put your finished layouts into the protectors, back to back. These albums can be extended by using extension posts. They make it easiest to rearrange the order of your layouts and are my favourite.

The most popular size of album is 30.5 x 30.5cm (12 x 12in). Most cardstock and paper is cut to that size. Smaller albums are available in 21.6 x 28cm (8½ x 11in), 20.3 x 20.3cm (8 x 8in) and 15.2 x 15.2cm (6 x 6in). These make good gift albums.

For a Christmas album you can choose one of an appropriate colour or finish. Some companies make albums specifically decorated for Christmas. If you cannot find one that you like, you could decorate the cover yourself.

Albums come in a variety of styles and sizes. Choose one to suit your photographs and personal style.

Paper

Cardstock is the mainstay of your album. It is cut to size to fit your album but usually comes in 30.5 x 30.5cm (12 x 12in). This is what you use as the background for your layouts, the mats for your photographs, embellishments and mini-books. Make sure it is not too thick – 160g is best. It must be acid and lignin free as it will come into direct contact with your photographs. Keep a variety of colours on hand.

Christmas **printed papers** come in a huge variety of colours and patterns to complement your cardstock and it is largely down to personal taste which ones you choose. They range from traditional colours and motifs to bright and geometric designs. They can be combined or used individually. Christmas paper ranges often include beautiful music or script papers. Whichever ones you choose, do not let the patterns detract from your photographs.

If the budget allows for a few **specialist papers**, embossed, gold blocked, handmade, silk papers or vellums are always an attractive addition to a Christmas page.

Embellishments

There is a vast array of embellishments to choose from. The skill is matching them up with your photographs and papers but not overpowering them.

Rub-on transfers come as individual letters, words or images. They are easily applied to your layout and will adhere to a variety of surfaces. **Sequins** can be stitched or stuck on and add a bit of glitz. **Metal eyelet charms**, **tags** and **frames** can be used as they are or they can be altered with acrylic paint or transfers. **Beads** can be used individually or strung on to your layout.

Acrylic embellishments come in a variety of colours and shapes and give your page a modern look. **Chipboard embellishments** tend to have a more traditional look. **Bottle caps** are a fun novelty. They are available plain or printed, and you can embellish them yourself. They need to be attached using thick **3D foam squares**.

Eyelets are useful for all pages and there is a huge variety of colours, sizes and shapes. Use them functionally to attach layers or as decoration.

Slide mounts are either plastic or card. Use them as they are or cover them to match your colour scheme. They are useful to frame other embellishments or significant sections of your photographs. **Faux film strip** makes a lovely border or can be cut into individual sections and used with the slide mounts.

Ribbons can be wrapped, tied, woven or made into bows or flowers. **Die-cuts** and **cardstock stickers** are often available to match your chosen papers. **Christmas decorations** are a useful source of inspiration. I always watch for small, flat decorations in the winter sales. The stationery cupboard can hold unexpected treasures such as **mini bulldog clips** and coloured and legal **paper clips**. **Buttons** come in a variety of colours and shapes and are easily attached.

Other materials

A **heating tool** is used with **embossing powders, ink** and **watermark pads.** **Foam** and **rubber stamps**, especially alphabet ones, are useful for titles and journaling. They can be used with **acrylic paints. Inkpads** are useful in a selection of colours – you will use black the most. Metallic inkpads add a festive touch to Christmas pages. **Chalk inkpads** will add soft colour and can be applied to give an aged look to embellishments.

A **cork mat** and **piercing tool** are used to punch holes safely for stitching on pages or joining pages in mini-books.

An **eyelet tool kit** is invaluable. It consists of a setting mat, hammer, hole punch and setter. Most have interchangeable heads to accommodate different sizes of eyelet.

Craft punches are a quick way to add a simple embellishment to your layout. Save your paper scraps to use with them.

Label printers and **plastic tape** are making a comeback. The tape is available in a number of colours and the labels make useful sized journaling strips for names or dates.

Staples and a **stapler** are also useful. Some shops sell a variety of coloured staples.

3D foam squares can be used to adhere and raise die-cuts and other embellishments off the page to add some dimension to your layout.

Dimensional paints are available in a number of finishes. Pearlescent and metallic paints look lovely on Christmas pages.

Wire can be shaped and combined with buttons and beads.

Fancy-edged scissors can add a different look to paper and card edges.

You will also need some items to decorate. **Hardback notebooks** can be covered and embellished. These are available cheaply from most stationery shops. **Mason** or **button jars** can be labelled and filled with journaling strips. **Bindi tins** are fun to embellish and fill, and come in a variety of sizes. **Acrylic photo baubles** can be personalised with family photographs and decorated festively to hang on the tree.

A heating tool, foam stamps, a photo bauble, acrylic paints, gold wire, a Mason jar, a notebook, dimensional paint, coloured staples and a stapler, 3D foam squares, craft punches, rubber stamps, a watermark pad, embossing powder, a bindi tin, fancy-edged scissors, double-sided tape, a label printer and plastic tape, an eyelet tool kit, a piercing tool, cork mat and inkpads.

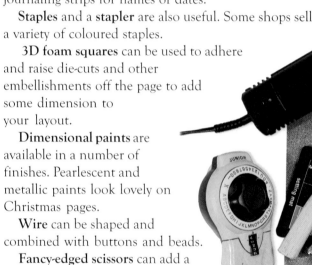

Techniques

There are a number of simple techniques that you will use on most of your scrapbooking pages.

Cropping

Cropping is the term used for cutting your photographs. This is done if you are not happy with the content or composition. We do not always take the perfect photograph and cropping will remove the empty spaces, the people we did not want, or those stray items that creep in at the edges.

However it is important that you do not remove all the background from photographs as you want to be able to set the scene and tell the story. Never cut polaroids as chemicals will leak out and spoil your page. Heritage photographs should be treated with respect as you are unlikely to have the negatives. Keep them whole to preserve historical detail. You can have photographs copied if you want to crop them.

Look carefully at your photographs. Choose five or six that you feel tell the story and focus on the theme of your layout. You do not have to crop all of your photographs. Do not get too carried away!

If you want to give your photographs a straight edge, use your guillotine to cut them. You can also use a template and scissors or a cutting system to cut them into circles or ovals.

All these photographs have benefited from being cropped.

Mistletoe
Try experimenting with different ways to crop.

Matting

Matting is the process of mounting your photographs on a coloured cardstock mat. This can add definition to your photograph, enhance the colours and add interest to the pages. Photographs can be matted in a number of different ways but the simplest is shown below.

  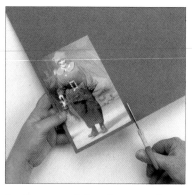

1. Apply adhesive to the back of your photograph using a repositionable tape runner as shown here. You can also use photo stickers.

2. Place the photograph on the cardstock, leaving an even border. To help you get it straight, line up the photograph with the machine-cut edge of the cardstock.

3. Cut round the photograph using scissors.

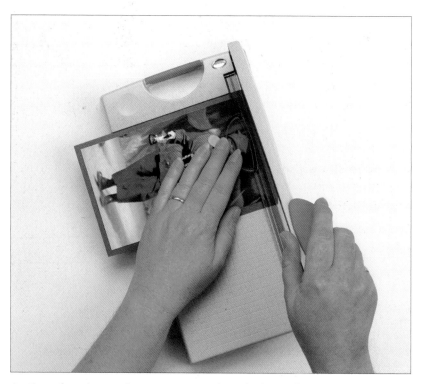

4. Complete the mat by trimming neatly with the guillotine.

Ivy
You can double mat the photograph for added impact.

Granny's hat
Mat a section of the photograph to bring attention to a particular point.

Choosing colour

Choosing colours for your page is a very personal thing. We all have our favourite colour palettes, and choosing the right colours is the key to a good page. Colour creates the mood and often enhances the photograph. A new scrapbooker often worries about choosing colours but ultimately you must go with what pleases you and your personality.

When creating a layout, there are two simple ways to choose your colours: firstly being led by the colours in the photographs. By looking at the photographs you can often select colours that match or complement those you can see. In the example shown on the right I have chosen two shades of blue from the jackets worn in the photograph, and one of grey. I chose the grey because I wanted a light colour but the white was too bright and would not allow the photographs to stand out. Secondly, we can choose colour by considering the theme of the layout. People tend to associate particular colours with events, celebrations, moods or seasons. Christmas is traditionally associated with red, green and gold. There are, however, lots of different shades and tones of these colours.

Rosie's first snow
The colour choice has been led by the photograph. I have looked at the clothes and the background to choose cardstock and embellishments.

The best one is at the bottom
The colour choice has been led by the theme. I have chosen red, green and gold – traditional Christmas colours.

I have used the same photograph in two similar layouts shown below to illustrate how different colours can alter the mood of the layout.

It is best to start with two colours, one for the background and one for the mats. Other colours can then be added in with embellishments or patterned papers. Lay the photograph on both colours to decide which way round looks best. A very light or dark photograph can be transformed by the colour you choose to mat it on. A dark photograph can be lifted with a light mat and a very light photograph can be muted on a dark mat. The coloured mat will also define the edges of the photograph and make it stand out on the page.

A holly jolly Christmas

I printed the photograph in colour and have chosen red and green, but in bright non-traditional shades to give a very modern look. I have complemented this with bright, funky stickers and printed papers

Jingle bells

I have printed the picture in sepia and softened the edges. Again I have chosen red and green but this time in darker shades with a weathered look. This is complemented with chipboard word tiles. The overall look is more traditional.

15

Layout

The first thing you need to decide is whether you are creating a single or double-page layout. This will be influenced by how many photographs you have to use and how you arrange them. There is no correct number of photographs. It is not unusual to create a layout from a single photograph or to capture an event in ten to twelve photographs. Be led by how many photographs you have taken. You might like to produce an entire album of Christmas photographs every year or you may have a Christmas album that contains a layout from each year. Apart from photographs, you will also need to think about placement of a title, journaling and embellishments and arranging them to create a balanced layout.

There is usually a logical sequence for a series of photographs of an event: they make most sense if they are arranged chronologically. There may be one photograph that is a key focus and that should be given predominance.

Sometimes a layout can take time to put together; at other times it all comes together very quickly. Be patient and do not always strive for the perfect page – enjoy your scrapbooking.

A visit from Santa

I have used eight photographs on this layout but have spaced them so as not to make the page look overcrowded. The layout is balanced because in terms of shapes, each page is a mirror image of the other. I have not over-embellished the layout because the photographs themselves are very busy.

Jake's first Christmas
A very simple layout with only three photographs arranged in a circle. The embellishment is again kept to a minimum because of the busy, colourful photographs.

Let it snow
If you have a particular photograph that you like, have it printed larger and use it as the main focus for a layout.

Journaling

Journaling is the documenting of facts or feelings on your pages. It helps you to remember and to tell the story to others looking at your album whether now or in the future. You can write as little or as much as you want to, but do write something. It is a good prompt to use the four Ws: who, what, when and where? This is useful historical documentation for future generations. Include your family traditions, favourite Christmas carols or poems, a list of your presents, funny or sad stories and what you ate for dinner.

There are lots of different ways to journal and it is nice to incorporate a variety in your album.

Using foam stamps and acrylic paint

These are great for creating a quick title.

1. Spread the paint out on a flat tray using an old paintbrush.

2. Press the foam stamp in the paint and stamp the cardstock.

25.12.04
Use the date as your title.

Concertina envelopes

Using envelopes to hold your journaling is a great way of hiding very personal thoughts or including a lot of journaling that would have taken up too much space on your page.

1. Apply repositionable tape to the inside of the flap of the first envelope.

2. Stick the front (the side you would address) of the next envelope to the flap.

3. Stick all the envelopes together in the same way. They can then be folded up and attached to your layout with the journaling inside.

Letters to Santa

I copied my children's letters to Santa before they sent them up the chimney, to include in my layout. I thought they would enjoy showing them to their own children in the future.

Using hinges

This is another great way to include hidden journaling. Create a hinged section on your layout and conceal the journaling below it.

1. Use eyelet tools and a setting mat to make a hole in the card and place an eyelet through the hinge.

2. Set the eyelet as shown. Attach the other side of the hinge to your background.

A cold and frosty morning

Under the main picture there is another photograph and some writing about our Boxing Day walk. This is revealed when the photograph is lifted on the hinges.

Text boxes

It is very easy to create text boxes using your computer and you can make up your own word definitions to journal on your page. The definitions can include things that are pertinent to your family. This is often a lot easier than writing straight prose.

Christmas
1. 25th December 2. excited children 3. exchanging gifts 4. turkey dinner 5. all the family together 6. snow 7. celebration 8. stockings hung

Eyelets, snaps and brads

These all have both functional and decorative uses in scrapbooking. They come in a variety of colours, shapes and sizes. There are many special ones for Christmas: snowflakes, stars, trees, decorations, holly and poinsettias.

Setting eyelets or snaps

3. Turn the card over and use the hammer and the setter this time to set the eyelet or snap in the hole.

1. Place the card on the setting mat and use the hole punching tool and hammer to make a hole for the eyelet or snap.

2. Place the eyelet or snap in the hole.

Winter days
The snowflake eyelets on this layout are purely decorative.

Christmas concert
Eyelets are very useful for attaching vellum. Printed vellum has been placed over a photograph to use as the title block on the layout. The photograph was slightly out of focus, but once the vellum is placed on top, this is not noticeable.

Christmas mini-book
The eyelets here have a function – they hold the book together, whereas the brads are purely decorative.

Embellishments

Embellishments can make your page look extra special. They can be as simple or as complicated as you wish. Try not to over-embellish; remember the photographs are the most important elements on the page. There is an endless list of embellishments with a Christmas theme: buttons, stickers, die cuts, rub-on transfers, flowers, bottle caps and more.

Using rub-on transfers

Rub-on transfers are easy to use and come in a variety of designs including lettering and images. They can be used on different surfaces.

1. Cut out a rub-on transfer from the sheet.

2. Line up the shape on a metal tag and rub it carefully with a lolly stick applicator.

3. Peel off the backing and the transfer will be stuck to the tag.

When using letter transfers, rub on the last letter of the word first, as shown. Then complete the word. This way, you avoid running out of space once you have started.

Using slide mounts and faux film strips

I love using slide mounts. They come in a variety of colours but you can cover them with paper to match your layout. Here I have combined them with faux film strips.

1. Stick a strip of white card to the cardstock using repositionable tape.

2. Stick the faux film strip on top using a glue pen. The colours will show up well because they are laid over the white card. Add a slide mount stuck down with glue dots.

Noel

A pre-printed bottle cap makes an unusual embellishment for this page. You can also decorate your own.

Rosie's first Christmas

A floral Christmas decoration was taken apart and reassembled to make it flatter on the page. This adds a very feminine touch to the page. It was attached with glue dots.

Presents

Use pre-printed embellishments to make decorating your pages very easy. These are cardstock stickers that make your pages look three-dimensional when they are in fact totally flat.

23

DECORATING THE TREE

You will need

Cardstock, one sheet of red and one of light green, 30.5 x 30.5cm (12 x 12in)

Patterned paper with a Christmas theme, 30.5 x 30.5cm (12 x 12in)

Photograph

Guillotine

Scissors

Foam letter stamps

Heating tool

Chalk inkpad, dark green

Embossing inkpad, clear

Embossing powder, gold

Scrap paper

3D foam squares

Label printer and plastic tape

Repositionable tape

This activity is eagerly awaited by my children every year. They all have their favourite decorations that they want to hang and each one can only reach up to a certain height. I like to take photographs that capture their childish innocence and their awe at the beauty and magic of the tree.

1. Use the guillotine to cut the patterned paper to 15 x 25cm (6 x 9⅞in).

2. Tear three of the edges, tearing towards you to expose the white core of the paper. Leave one of the long sides untorn.

3. Brush a dark green chalk inkpad over the torn edges. Brush the edges of the red cardstock with the same colour. Cut a 23 x 20cm (9 x 7⅞in) light green cardstock mat for the photograph and ink its edges in the same way.

4. Press a foam letter stamp on to the embossing inkpad.

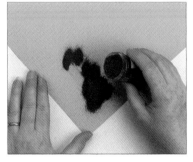

5. Stamp on to the light green cardstock, then sprinkle gold embossing powder on the letter.

6. Pour the excess powder off on to a piece of folded scrap paper. It can then be returned easily to the pot.

7. Heat the letter with a heating tool until the gold is raised and shiny.

8. Cut round the letter using scissors.

9. Trim close to the letter, using the guillotine and leaving an even border.

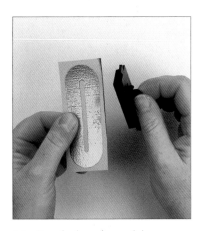

10. Brush the edges of the cut-out letter using the dark green chalk inkpad.

11. Stick 3D foam squares to the back of the letter. Make all the letters of the word 'WONDER' in the same way.

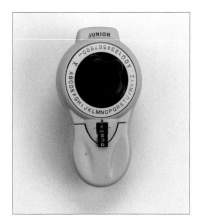

12. Print out the child's name using the label printer. Assemble all the elements on the red cardstock as shown opposite.

Wonder

Duncan loved the Christmas tree this year. He added some decorations he had made at school and could often be found sitting looking at the lights.

Going to buy the tree with Granny and Grampa
The page is decorated with a shaker box containing sequins and buttons.

Give

Take close-up photographs of favourite decorations. Try capturing yourself on a glass bauble so that you, the photographer, can be included on a layout. To avoid flare, do not use a flash.

FOOD AND DRINK

You will need

Small ring-bound concertina journal

A selection of patterned papers with a kitchen/food theme, 30.5 x 30.5cm (12 x 12in)

A selection of cardstock to match

PVA glue

Paintbrush

Craft knife and cutting mat

Scissors

Stapler and coloured staples

Double-sided tape

Repositionable tape

Small letter stamps

Inkpad

Coloured paper clips and mini bulldog clips

Coloured ribbon to match cardstock and patterned papers

Food and drink always play an important role in celebrations and this is never truer than at Christmas. Share your family food traditions with future generations by recording them in an album or a mini-book. This is a small recipe journal that you can pass round to friends and ask them to contribute a favourite Christmas recipe that is special to their family.

Tip

Choose a ring-bound journal with a large wire binding. This will make it easier to fit in pages that have become bulky when embellished.

1. Carefully remove the ring binder from your journal.

2. Cut a piece of patterned paper so that it is at least 3cm (1¼in) wider than the journal cover all the way round. Cover evenly with PVA glue diluted with water to the consistency of single cream.

3. Stick the cover of the journal to the glued paper. Press flat.

4. Trim all round the edges of the journal cover, leaving a narrow border. Cut across the corners as shown, 3mm (⅛in) from the album cover's corners.

5. Fold the edges over and stick them down as shown. Do not worry if your cover looks a little wrinkled when it is wet. It will flatten out to a snug fit as it dries.

6. To remake the holes, use a craft knife to cut squares in the top layer of paper, then cut an 'x' in the bottom layer and fold back the triangles.

8. Cut a 11 x 4.5cm (4⅜ x 1¾in) piece of mid-brown cardstock, tear one long side and stick it to the first page. Cut a piece of patterned paper 9 x 12cm (3½ x 4¾in), tear three of the edges and apply repositionable tape to the back.

7. Finish off the inside with a 11.8 x 16.5cm (4⅝ x 6½in) piece of the same paper. Remake the holes as above.

9. Stick the patterned paper on top of the brown cardstock as shown.

10. Apply repositionable tape to a 5cm (2in) length of ribbon.

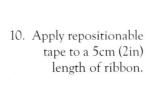

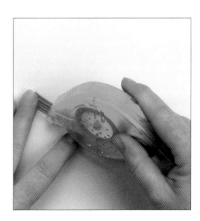

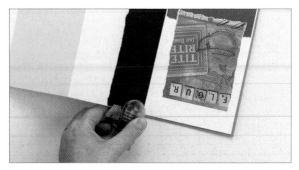

11. Fold the ribbon into a 'v' shape.

12. Apply a little repositionable tape to the back of the 'v'.

13. Stick a 6 x 16.3cm (2$\frac{3}{8}$ x 6$\frac{3}{8}$in) piece of dark brown cardstock, torn along one long edge, to the second page. Staple the ribbon to the edge of the page using a copper-coloured staple.

14. Staple on a second ribbon 'v' as shown. Continue decorating the journal pages with collaged card, paper and embellishments. Journaling can be added using a printer or small letter stamps. Brush the torn edges of some pieces of paper with an inkpad to add an aged look.

15. To make an additional page insert, cut a piece of dark brown card to 16.9 x 9cm (6$\frac{5}{8}$ x 3$\frac{1}{2}$in). Fold the two short sides together. Measure 1.5cm ($\frac{5}{8}$in) from the middle crease and crease again on one side.

16. Add a torn patterned paper edge to your insert on the shortest side with repositionable tape. Place double-sided tape down the length of the 1.5cm ($\frac{5}{8}$in) width spine and stick it to a left-hand page of the album, up to the crease. You now have extra surfaces to decorate or journal on.

17. Add a mini bulldog clip and a paper clip as shown.

The finished recipe journal – the perfect way of sharing Christmas food traditions with friends, and with future generations.

Stir Up Sunday
On the first Sunday of
Advent we make our
Christmas Pudding. We
use a recipe that is 150
years old and has a secret
ingredient – stout.
We stir sixpences in to the
mixture and make a wish.

Stir up Sunday

Even though the children do not actually like eating Christmas pudding, they are always keen to help me make it. I have made this layout with some close-up photographs of the pudding ingredients (I used the macro setting on my camera) and some pictures of the finished pudding on Christmas day. I have created a shadow box on the right-hand page by sandwiching foam core between two layers of cardstock and cutting a recess in which I have laid a spoon. The layout is decorated with silver sixpences which I won on an internet auction.

THE NATIVITY PLAY

You will need

Four sheets of olive green cardstock, 30.5 x 30.5cm (12 x 12in)

Two sheets of light green cardstock, 30.5 x 30.5cm (12 x 12in)

One sheet of beige cardstock, 30.5 x 30.5cm (12 x 12in)

Two sheets of kraft-coloured corrugated card, 28 x 21.5cm (11 x 8½in)

Nine square buttons in different colours and sizes

Two silver 3mm (⅛in) silver eyelets

Eyelet tool kit

Green ribbon

Glue dots

Repositionable tape

Piercing tool and cork mat

Darning needle

Stranded cotton, ecru

Guillotine

Photographs

Drawings

If you have young children or grandchildren, nothing can beat going to see them in a nativity play. I cry every time. I have captured my son in his minor role as a cow and used those photographs as the main emphasis for this double-page layout. The other photographs I took have been included in a mini-book along with some pictures that my children drew to illustrate the Christmas story.

1. Apply glue dots to the back of the photographs so that they can be matted on corrugated card.

2. Mat both photographs, making sure the lines of the corrugated card go the same way.

3. Use glue dots again to stick the matted photographs to the light green cardstock.

Tip

To print text on to the card or paper you are using for your titles and journaling, first print out the text on standard A4 printer paper. Apply repositionable tape to the back of the item you wish to print on. Fix it over the text, making sure it is secure. Run the paper back through the printer, overprinting on to the item. Then you can peel off the item and rub off the adhesive.

4. Print out the title and journaling on the beige card. Cut the card round the journaling to 13 x 10cm (5⅛ x 4in) and tear the bottom as shown. Stick the journaling in place using repositionable tape.

5. Cut the title to 5 x 9cm (2 x 3½in) and tear the bottom. Stick it down as shown. Attach the buttons using glue dots. This completes the left-hand page of the layout.

6. To make a mini-book for the right-hand page, cut three pieces of olive green cardstock 30.5 x 15cm (12 x 5⅝in) and fold them in half to make a spine. Open them out on a cork mat and use a piercing tool to make three holes in the spine, 2cm (¾in), 7.5cm (3in) and 13cm (5⅛in) from the top of the mini-book.

7. Stitch the spine using six strands of embroidery thread and a darning needle. Come up from the back in hole 2, leaving a 7.5cm (3in) tail. Go down in hole 1, come back up through hole 2 and go down in 3.

8. Come back up through hole 2, take the thread under the stitch each side to anchor it and go back down in hole 2.

9. Trim the end and tie it to the tail you left at the beginning.

10. Print the title, trim the card to 9.6 x 9cm (3¾ x 3½in) and tear the bottom. Stick it to the mini-book using repositionable tape. Stick on the buttons using glue dots.

The finished layout. Duncan was so pleased to be a cow. He wanted to wear his costume all the time, especially as the nose, when pressed, made a very realistic 'moo'.

11. Scan or photocopy some children's drawings on the Nativity theme, reduce them to size and tear the edges, and stick them in to the mini-book with matted photographs, using repositionable tape.

12. Attach the mini-book to a corrugated card mat using glue dots, and attach this to the cardstock. Use an eyelet hole punch to make holes in the cardstock, one either side of the matted book, and set eyelets. Thread a ribbon through the holes and tie a bow.

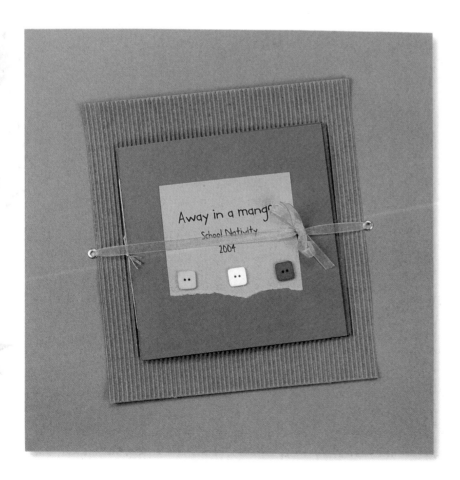

Jake gives his list to Santa

A very simple layout using one picture. The edges of the layout and the metal embellishments have been dry brushed with white acrylic paint.

Reindeer Food
oats to eat
&
glitter to guide
the way

Reindeer food
Another family tradition is sprinkling glittery oats on Christmas Eve to guide in the reindeer.
The memory saver on the page contains sequins, glitter and cut-up paper, to look like oats.

MEMORY GIFT

You will need

A hardback notebook

One sheet of Christmas patterned paper, 30.5 x 30.5cm (12 x 12in)

One sheet of dark green printed paper, 30.5 x 30.5cm (12 x 12in)

One sheet of pink/red cardstock, 30.5 x 30.5cm (12 x 12in)

Double-sided tape

Mason jar

Pink ribbon

PVA glue and paintbrush

Glue dots

Repositionable tape

Corner rounder

A journal jar is a very special present. It consists of a decorated jar filled with pieces of paper that have questions printed on them. A question is picked from the jar every day and stuck into a decorated journal, where the answer to the question is then written. The questions should evoke memories from the past that can be written down for future generations. It is the ideal present for a child to give to a grandparent. When the journal is full, it is given back to the child so that he or she can share the memories. The questions could be about childhood, school days, holidays and of course, Christmas.

1. Water down PVA glue to the consistency of single cream and brush it over the back of a sheet of Christmas patterned paper. Stick the paper to the book's cover.

2. Cut across the corners as shown and fold down the excess paper.

3. Open up the book so that the spine bulges open as shown. Cut the covering paper into a flap at the spine and tuck it into the opening.

4. Apply PVA glue to the endpaper.

5. Press the book flat to stick the endpaper to the front cover. Do not worry if the endpaper is wrinkled while the glue is wet; it will flatten as it dries.

6. Cut out a tag from pink cardstock and print instructions on it (see the tip on page 37). Make a ribbon decoration as shown on page 32. Stick the ribbon to the tag. Layer torn rectangles of pink cardstock and green patterned paper and stick the ribboned tag on top.

7. Print the instructions for the journal jar on to pink cardstock and tear round the edges, making sure you tear towards you. Stick the instructions to the inside front cover using repositionable tape.

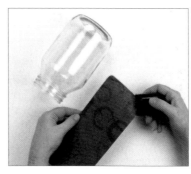

8. For the jar's label, cut a 22 x 9.3cm (8⅝ x 3⅝in) rectangle from green patterned paper and round off the corners using a corner rounder.

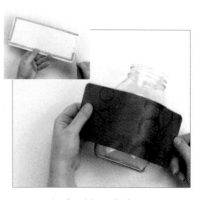

9. Apply double-sided tape to the back of the label and stick it to the jar.

10. Print the second label on pink cardstock, round off the corners and use repositionable tape to stick it to the back of the jar.

Tip

Look for suitable fonts to use on your labels. There are many fonts that you can download from the internet.

11. Make the title in the same way and stick it to the green label.

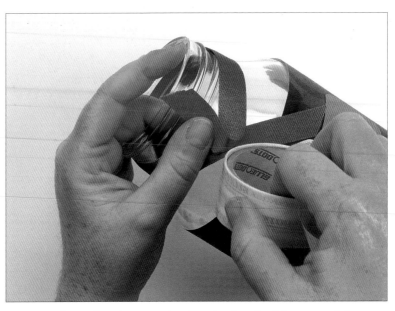

12. Use a large glue dot to stick a length of pink ribbon round the neck of the jar. Trim the ends to match.

13. Print questions on pink cardstock. Cut them up into individual pieces, roll them up and place them in the jar.

Tip

Here are some ideas for questions:

What are your first memories of Christmas?

What was your favourite Christmas present?

Did you hang up a stocking and what did you get in it?

Do you remember a particular Christmas?

Did it always snow at Christmas?

Once you start thinking about it, you will come up with lots of questions yourself.

Opposite

The finished memory gift. This makes a lovely present for a grandparent. Encourage your children to help write the questions. They will be enthralled by the answers.

Bindi boxes

Memories do not always have to be recorded on a page. I have used this tin of bindi boxes to store some Christmas memories. Photographs, trinkets and words can be used to sum up a special celebration. The vintage images on the inside of the box lid were taken from a collection of old cards found at a charity shop.

Photo bauble

Photo baubles are another way of storing and displaying Christmas memories. They can be decorated on the outside with rub-on transfers and a selection of bright ribbons. Make a new one each year to decorate your tree.

Index

Cookies for Santa

Every Christmas Eve the children make cookies to leave out for Santa along with his whiskey and Rudolph's carrot. This layout shows the step-by-step process of making them. On the left-hand page, the torn red and green cardstock has been stitched together and folded back. The cookies on the border have been made from cork and decorated with pearlised dimensional paint and bead sprinkles.